AF255744

NEW ZEALAND
POEMS · PICTURES · PROSE

LYRICAL
RAZOR · BLADES

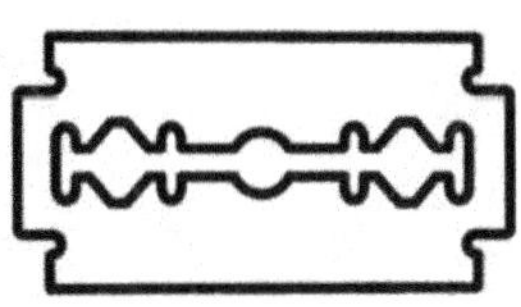

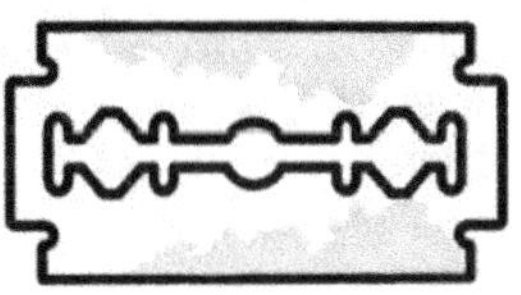

JOHN & ALEX
STRINGER

Published by *Maiden New Zealand*.
Printed in the USA by *IngramSpark*.
Text © John C. Stringer & Alexander T. Stringer
as denoted (55) or (25) throughout text.
Production & artwork © John Stringer 2019.

Edition 1, hardcover and eBook.
December 2019.
Christchurch, New Zealand. 2019.

ISBN: 978-0-473-50562-2
Epub: 978-0-473-50561-5

2019
CHRISTCHURCH
NEW ZEALAND

*"There's no clear sign
  to tell the quality of a man.
Nature and place turn vice and virtue
  upside down.
I've seen a noble father breed
  a worthless son
And good sons come
  of evil parents."*

~ Euripides' *Orestes.*

"With lyrical razor blades!"

~ Alex Stringer's *Social Justice Warrior,* p. 22.

55/25

John (aged 55) and Alex Stringer (age 25) in 2018/19 are father and son living in Christchurch, New Zealand.

John, a published novelist, author and illustrator. Alex a rap-off champion and singer songwriter.

Their first collaboration of literary lyrical and pictographic ensembles.

This book was produced on a keyboard without periods or commas (which had to be cut and pasted) because Alex spilt beer on his Pa's *MacBook Air*. It nearly ended there, rated up there with his brother's removal of roof tiles (stacked nicely in a pile on the roof) so he could get inside the locked house to play *Playstation* after school. Only noticed a week later while mowing the back lawn ahead of rain.

Coincidental t-shirt selection, suggesting aesthetics might be serendipitously genetic.

Contents

The Works

19 works John Stringer   (55)
17 works Alex. Stringer (25)
 1 work   James Stringer (10).

Hudson Lost

Long narrow caverns of stone and steel
    –welts across the Hudson landscape.
Descending sun creeps down, her scarlet fingers
    Gently creep, to caress the cold hard of the streets.

Reminiscent of a softer day,
    Bisons' hooves upon the mossy morn,
Breath misting in the cold off a vigorous and fresh land,
    New from the crafting of God,

A virgin embrace gathering the teaming lives of America.

Gone are the hooves, the geese,
    The drumbeat of Cherokee,
Choked by the market shrill of the Money-bird,
    Alighted on every corner, in every transient face.

The sound of millions of wheels groaning through
    Ceaseless Promethean revolutions
On the asphalt tablecloth
    Of New York city.

Talkback radio, neon sermons, cacophony of cabs
    –Yellow buzzards swarming over the city carcass –
Roller-blades, crisply scything Central Park Avenue
    –The gasping lungs, decaying core of Big Apple.

And descending sun creeps gently down, her scarlet fingers
    Creep, caressing the cold hard of the street,
To wipe away the tears, of Hudson lost,
    Man way laid, and what appeared before.

~ (55) 1 September 1994 while living in Manhattan.

Mother Patriotic

Our mother never sleeps,
She smiles, she weeps,
She sounds like silence.

But we hate her,
We constantly rape her.
Bred with violence!

The older she gets,
The more we forget.
We are not quite giants.

One day she'll die.
People will cry.
We will stand defiant.

Mother Nature we love you!

~ (25) txt. ~ (55) pxt. 2017.

Alex's First Rap-off

Son Alex cleans out
    all the homies at his first big rap bout
        competition.

With some sweet rappin' scrappin'
    homie debris wreckin'
        word-cappin.'

Zand the C-City Kiwi *Eminem* breaks freer
    and slays the qu-eer
        L.A.-aping wannabee gansta A-City rapper.

Drivin' o'er them with lit-er-ary tract-ors,
    as his main reac-tor,
        Into which he fac-tors, his gang-stirs.

~ (55) 2016.

"Homie"- friend, local companion.
"Gansta" - alternative of "gangster."
"Zand" - Alex(Zand)er.
"Word-cappin'" - shooting words like bullets, as in 'capping' someone.
"C-City" - Christchurch; "A-City" - Auckland, New Zealand.
"Gang-stirs" a play on rap mockery of LA-esque Auckland gangsters.

Own Grind

I ain't focused on what the rest do.
These rappers act as if they' created in a test tube.
Al Stringer got the finesse too.

They don't wanna see a rapper like me let loose,
I'm gonna get it in, though.
I'll be bumping trash sh-t out the win-dow.

I fill my sh-t up to the brim, ho.
Hollow? Sh-t same colour as a fla-min-go.
That's the life of me in Cheech. Zam brick.

Just tryin' ta find a piece.
Ah Yo! They wanna hear me preach.
I ain't been in the kitchen busy cookin' peach.

Thinkin' about them old times, when it's show time.
People talkin', ain't focussin' on their Own Grind!
I never mind o' what they make of that.

I just wanna rhyme and watch my paper stack.
I don't ride a same wave as a rap-boy.
Now they see me spazzin' on the trap, boy.

I'm just focused on my Own Grind!
I never been trendy like the kids in the scene.
I never gave a f**k about havin' designer jeans.
My pen been cre-atin' flames, I kept it supreme.
I got more lines than a coffee table at Charlie Sheen's.
They always like holy sh-t, ille-git.

"Yo! That boy can spit! About to flip sh-t!"
Haven't met me, they run their lip,
get a grip, all I do is spit. I show them dip

It's gonna be the way it go, though.
Your life good if you live it drama-free, yo!
One day you'll be celebrating at the t-o.

Yeah, hit the battles scene and catch a three-O.
They doubt hard. Al-Stringer, fin-er be the spitter-outta
Ta out last.

I don't give a f**k about bein' cool,
But you're my outcast.
I remember a time where it used to be belt-bast.

I don't ride a same wave as a rap-boy.
Now they see me spazzin' on the trap, boy.
I'm just focused on my Own Grind!
I'm just focused on my Own Grind!

~ (25). August 2017.

Hear audio: https://youtu.be/gx2EOeVF2_k

"Own Grind" - my own thing, *raison detré.*

"Bumping trash sh-t out the window" - spinning really good rap lyrics.

"Cheech" - Christchurch as in "Chch" or "C-City."

"Spazzin'" - acting spastic, 'going hard out,' energetic.

"Paper stack" - money growing like at a card game.

"Three-0" - 3-nil rap contest decision.

OWN
GRIND
AI STRINGER

"How Would Owning the Lakefront Dream Home Change your Life?"

A *Rye, Westchester* rabbi with a passion for Chinese food and a flight from New Zealand to New York CHANGED EVERYTHING. *Tuesdays with Morrie* – Rabbi Rothman taught a Kiwi husband about life, love and Peking Duck before an American girl was swept into the Pacific.

We wallowed in the lusciousness of humanity found in respective NZ and NY swathes: colour, people, food; broadening brushstrokes on Antipodean-New York palettes.

She regaled him with childhood pleasures of Reichards Lake, NY, and he of NZ Maori, *moa* and *morepork*. We shared the pleasures of places shattered by the 2010/11 New Zealand earthquakes. Our children scattered too– across three countries, three grandchildren.

We've come back a few times, bringing our children to walk through Chinatown, Soho, around the feet of *Liberty*, to eat '*hawt dawgs'* lawst in Central Park.

Lakefront lake light, though, recalling NZ *Wakatipu* and NY *Reichards*, would gather us home where we can paint, write and walk in the leaves of final careers, gathering again children and grandchildren to come to be; soak up our *New Yorks*; perhaps frame their own, amidst glimpses of past and future, sculpted together by North Atlantic/South Pacific chiseled winds of heart and hope.

~ (55) 2016.

Unsent entry to a New York Catskills lake cottage real estate purchase by skills competition.

ISIS Swag
["This is for all you Western dogs"]

Eye-iiii-sis, we are quite a cri-sis.
Eye-iiii-sis, there is no one like us!

Lace my four-year-old daughter's school bag with C4
So I can detonate it and blow the pre-school.
You be lookin' at me like I be evil,
I'm just doing what god wanted for my peo-ple.

I've got RPGs I've got M-16s,
I got all of these explosives and weapon-ry.
Do not f**k with me or I will be-head you in the street!
I'm swaggerin' it in my new sandals and my robe is *Versace*.

Eye-iiii-sis, who is gonna fight us?
Alla-lal-la-la-la-ah.

I think I'm ready to go.
I have to meet 72 virgins back at the promised land.
I'm goin' home and it's all in the name
Of the prophet Mohammed and

Eye-iiii-sis, who is gonna fight us?
Eye-iiii-sis, we are quite a cri-sis [BANG BANG!]

~ (25) August 2017.

See video: https://youtu.be/gt4NYY2mZU8

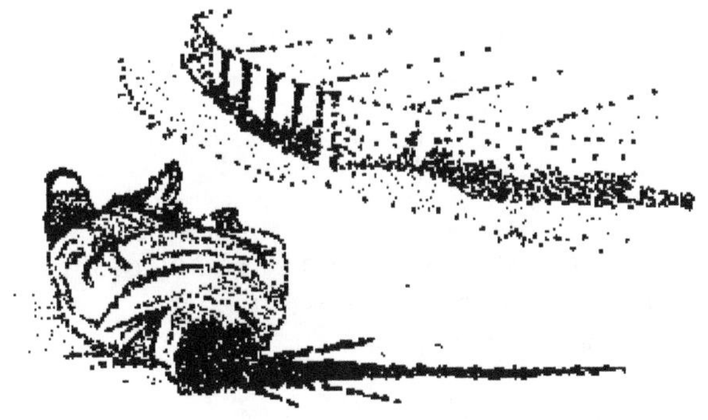

Tomorrow Sailing

Oh life, undone, life untied.
Long nights of quiet tears
With melancholy
At my side.

Like the solitary chime of kingfisher;
Blue/green flash across palette of green.
Life has become a single twanging strain.
Gone the warmth, the laughter,
The bustle of love, heart and hearth.

Bowed now,
Traipsing alone through this
Alleyway of change.
Years of goodness gone, goodness knows where. Not all.
Long investment –bankrupt, to leave
The strain of solitariness, unnoticeably unknown groaning.

What is life but a solo tango through
An empty dance hall;
The curdled milk of human kindness
Run dry.
Like sand on the tongue. This life undone,
Is a wrestling with the past,
To break free and sail with…

Tomorrow.

~ (55) ca 2015.

*"Here I lie mournful with desire, feeble in bitterness
        Of the pain, the gods inflicted upon me,
Stuck through the bones of love."*

~ Archilocus, *Poems*, ca. 640 BC.

Raw Sixty-Four

You wanna hear me spit some bars? Okay, okay.
It's the raw sixty-four!
I feel like I be one on the grates,
I wanna be remembered when I'm at the Gates.
That's why I'm slavin,' tryin' ta get my paper straight,
So I can fly out to Rome, buy an estate.

If you ain't with a good buzz, I don't relate,
I just elevate and I celebrate.
But I'll still make a hater back flip.
Another *"Oh, he dissin' me cos he ain't about the trap sh-t."*
We used to rap in a garage and set the bomb bay
And might be smashed by the time we had to get on st-age.
Reminisce and it gets me missin' them gone days.
But I look at my life now, but damn
we came a long-ways.

F**kin' around with a beast!
Even when I was a kid, they used to call me *"the Chief."*
I ain't got no time for the beef, I'm right in rollin' the leaf.
Makin' sure that my sh-t is poppin,' when they get released!
That's like, *"It's damn."* I make big moves,
I'm all about that. I'm like Trump.
I go ape sh-t on that stage, boy, I'm no chump!
I just be fillin' my cup, b-tch, I be snappin' out here
from the jump.

They talk about Stringer, but they know that my sh-t
Is always go Bump!

Sl-ow down though, I just like the way it sound, though.
You always said I'd never be sh-t.
But I was running by the time I hit the ground, though.
So come correct, if you wanna flex, boy, I'm chill,
I'm not really stressed, I'm just feelin' blessed.

Look around, I came up learnin' from the best.
I studied the art of finesse.
That is the reason they say I'm the best, aye.
I'm just out here tryin' to chase a double-u [W].
You gonna be hearing my sh-t when the summer's through.
I spit it raw
You never heard nobody this legit before.
It's Al Stringer with the raw sixty-four!

~ (25) 15 November 2017.

See video: https://youtu.be/dxAR3zwPqeM

"Double-u" [W] - a rip-off win.
"Raw sixty-four" - 64 lines of lyrical rap.
"Dissin'". - mocking, critising.
"Poppin'" - "Going off," happening eventfully.
"Snappin'" - Making it happen, doing it vigorously.

Treasury Foyer

Heart and soul came gushing, gushing.
      Like a burbling mountain stream
Racing, racing round the rocks,
      An un-orchestrated army of watery ants
Working to achieve,
      The goal at the bottom of the stream
–the tranquil pond. At peace.

Words came tumbling, tumbling.
      Like ugly boulders plunging, plunging, down
Into the pond, to leave
      Receding ripples of thought
For hours afterward.

~ (55) 22 October 1996.

Fragment 2

Victims queue outside adventure's halls
      "Nice to meet you Mr Provider,"
Loan me your sanity adventure calls.
      It's not the blacksmith it's the decider.

I met a man brought down to his knees
      "Here's a case with all my money."
Nowadays people are hard to please.
      I'm going to a place where skies are sunny.

~ (25). Date unknown.

Kaitorete Spit (Rakaia 2)

The sun at Rakaia Huts gleams in your eyes
      Except at twilight – when
As a melting orb it layers the rocks, the water,
      The driftwood, the scrub.

The sprawling shingle tangle of the riverbed, where
      In summer the lupins explode,
Hurling their seedy pay-load
      Onto the ground for ringnecks to gather.

They shrill intermittently from the tundra,
      –lightning flashes of brilliant colour
Amid the grey clay-powdered gorse
      And lupin 'down-the-back.'

The rabbits squat nervously, nibbling, ears alert.
      The terns and gulls reel.
A shadow, a trout, cruises menacingly in the
      Shrouded pool unaware of net or wader.

The jetboats, outboards and two-stroke roarers,
      Chortlers along Kaitorete Spit,
Spitting out the day's Urban Unwelcomes, who hoarsely rush
      And play across the country.

I retreat to the solitude and privacy
      Of the bush beyond the lagoon.
My turangawaewae –
      Soil and fern for soul to learn.

~ (55) ca 1990s.

"Ringnecks" - Mongolian ring-neck pheasant common in New Zealand.
"Turangawaewae" - (Maori) [tu-runga-why-why] a spiritual place to stand,
   place of identity.

Charles Philip Arthur George

Humbled by Crown, aloof,
Gordonstoun,
Death of Mountbatten

He walks dignified through streets of
Christ and Church
Future Head of Church and State

King to be crowned.
Thoughtful, wise, planted and grown
By heartache, trials, yet finding triumph

In realising a voice, amidst architecture,
Gardening and plants, pioneer of
Environment and conservation.

Helicopters, Australia, Goons, Polo,
Distilled now into dignity,
Maturity, consideration and endurance.

Like Joseph and Jeremiah in their wells,
Wales has endured his testings
And emerged in Cornwall, complete.

Ready to kneel in service to nation and Commonwealth
As we raise him up on plinth
Of Heritage, History and Hearth.

To take his Patient Patent Place
Among us as King
Determined by God.

He will give us his Head, but unlike Charles I,
We'll get his Heart
And learned Hindsight as well.

Go well Wales, we welcome you.
God save the Queen; God save the king.
God defend New Zealand.

~ 55, 23 November 2019

On the occasion of HRH and the Duchess of Cornwall's visit to Christchurch and New Zealand 17-23 November 2019, during which Prince Charles consented to become patron of the Christ Church cathedral rebuild and made a substantial donation to its restoration.

Water Aross Greywacke *(Rakaia 22)*

Now, the woman I danced with
In Life and Love and
Misunderstood
Is gone.
But I still reach out to her.

When I am alone
In the half light of a canyon,
Or silhouetted by twilight
Against the hues of majestic
Passing Rakaia,

As she
Winds down from the Alps to the Sea,
All existence seems to fade
In to a Being
Of Soul and Memories.

The sounds of the winter snow melt,
Tumbled across greywacke, and a four-count
Fly-casting rhythm,
Are my companions now, as we wait
For a fish to rise, a bulldog at my side.

This river was cut by the Great Flood and runs
Over rocks from the basement of Time.
Some of these rocks are timeless raindrops.
And under the rocks are the words
And some of the words are hers.

~ (55) ca 1990s.

*"The blacksmith of love has hammered me and crushed me
On his anvil and has plunged me in to a winter torrent."*

~ Anacreon of Teos, ca 500 BC.

Social Justice Warrior (SJW)

I wrote this song cos, Regressives can't see it.
They can't stand for nothing, they're politically paraplegic.
Constantly whinging about how they're a victim,
As if they breathe it.
Callin' people a racist or a bigot, but don't believe it.

And it's insane. I thought college students
Would be using their mem-brane.
And they're makin' teachers resign.
It's all in the name of free speech –if it is mine!
And patronising minorities makes 'em feel good inside.

And *Black Lives Matter* ain't exempt from this rhyme.
How many more seeds of racial hatred are you gonna plant,
In the minds of simple folk,
Who don't even know their own stance?
They sympathise with you, to show how racist they aren't,
While being racist.

Just listen to what they say,
Black Lives Matter are like the modern day KKK, kay!
Against white people and somehow it's okay.
I saw the co-founder spit racial hatred the other day.
She had taken to *Twitter* to say to Allah she prayed,
To give her strength not to murder any white people today.

But who cares though? If it had been a white male
Sayin' the same sh-t in reverse
He woulda lost his whole career, though.

This is an illustration of double standards.
Being hateful and racist will only ever bring trouble.
And it doesn't belong in this day and age
That's why I wage a war on these Regressives
With lyrical razor blades!

Boohoo hoo S-J-W.
Wicked white privilege, [wikkit] white privilege
Boohoo hoo S-J-W.
[Check-it] white privilege.

And these social justice warriors even persist
To pretend like these massive issues
I can't really fath-om, what position they're bent in?
Why is Islam a magic religion that never gets mentioned?

They don't debate you, they won't listen to reason.
They'll just insult you, screamin' what they believe in.
Kickin' and cussin,' bleedin' and even playin' them games,
Throwin' a temper tantrum, cryin' and callin' you names.

I even got called a "white supremacist,"
For goin' toe-to-toe with a Nazi feminist.
She said I got no right to define what racism is
Because I'm white
Guess what? That's "racism" b-tch!

It doesn't phase me, it does amaze me.
These Regressive drum-circle-dwelling hippies
Are flippin' cra-zy, and maybe,
In the future my ba-by, may need to deal with this.
Bubble-wrap society that they have made, see.

That's why I'm singin' this song
I can't put up with PC sh-t for too long.
I wrote this song cos, they can't see it.
They don't stand for nothing, they're politically paraplegic!

Boohoo hoo S-J-W, [check-it] white privilege.
Boohoo hoo S-J-W, [wikkit] white privilege.

~ (25) August 2017. See video: https://youtu.be/wzg7Ub_KSi0

"Flippin' a crazy" - 'going native,' going crazy as an over reaction.
"Wikkit" - rapper phonetic sound effect as in Scratch (record) DJ technique
   but here being used as a play alongside "wicked."
"Check-it" - Check it out, observe, played here with Wikkit/Wicked.

Cerberus

Cerberus!
You are a barking Shade!
I cleave you
      W'yon claymore o' Contempt!

For I am a Dust-man ...filled with Breath!
Smiting Fear amid Be-wilder-ment
      of Life, while you Guard
The eternal steps of Death!

~ (55) 1990s.

Cerberus, the hell dog that guards the gate of Hades (after William Blake).

2 Hate Malls

Walkin' through the Mall makes me a horrible per-son.
I want to murder everyone I s-ee.
Walkin' through the Mall makes me furious and cur-sin,'
That is the way it has always been.

Mall Rats are the worst, they make me whiter than albinos,
Pullin' gang signs and they are only thirteen.
Bucket hats and weed leaf socks, tucked into their *chinos*.
Wait right here while I grab my M16!

People that take so long to bloody order.
You should have decided when you were in the line.
So here ya go, here's a f***ing water.
So I hope you'll stop wasting all my time.

People who walk real slow and they won't let you pass them.
It ain't my fault you got not sh-t to do!
People who piss right next to me,
Even though there's twenty other urinals.

I'm gonna piss on your shoe.

~ (25) 30 August 2015.

See video: https://youtu.be/WG2vzrmnRSM

"Pullin' gang signs" - hand signals that represent a gang affiliation, such as
the Texas long horn/Devil's horns or the single extended finger "Up Yours"
or Agincourt's two bow fingers "giving the fingers" (to the French·knights).

Bland Drowning

Storming down Meadows of Moderation,
Plunging in to the boiling Gorge
of Extreme,

Drawing breath to con-tem-plate,
The battering of Body,
Soul and fractious Spirit,

Swam he to Infinity; towards the Edge,
Only to find there, dryness of Heart,
No purpose, No Horizon.

Plunged he, back, in to
The foaming embrace of Scylla,
To wrestle with Charybdis.

Yet alive and on Fire;
No simmering glow
For this restless Breast.

Bring on the Beasts!

~ (55) 2001.

"But it breaks my spirit; underneath my breast
All the heart is shaken.
...Fever shakes my body, paler I turn than glass!

~ Sappho, ca 500 BC.

"Charybdis" - from *The Odyssey* a whirlpool like monster next to Scylla.

Red Zone Battle Bars

Let me grab the mike, and crush those who oppose.
Step up on this b-tch and lookin' like Moses.
So tie down your damn Nan, brother! Cos Al Stringer's
In town and I'm down to bang grandmothers.

"Hi," f**kin', *"hi!"* I'm havin' fun with it.
I don't take it too serious, just rhyme with it.
Most of these rappers are talkin' guns with it.
I'll just rap about how sh-t I am at rappin,' till I'm done with it.

Just to distance my sh-t from whack fools,
All of these G's they tryna act cool.
They said I was a unique soul,
Cos I spat dope jams from my pram at two weeks old.

I'm the chief with this.
All I wanna be doin,' is snortin' cocaine
off a Mia Khalifa's bits
Al Stringer –Hell Bringer.

Got a drinkin' problem
And I really like to shelf pingers
With twelve
Ghing-ers.

~ (25) 30 August 2016.

See video: https://youtu.be/zd44cfD_rwY

"Ghingers" - people with red hair.
"Mia Khalifa" - porn star personality and websites.

Drugs-JT Mix

I really thought that I was livin' we-ll
Till I woke up in a prison cell.
They said that I was in the livin' room
Dancin' naked cos I'd taken 'shrooms.

Tryin' to hump whatever's next to me
Turns out I took too much *Ecstasy*.
Then I dropped a couple o' acid tabs
All they did was make me sh-t my pants.

Cos I didn't listen when they say
You really need to go and pay, aye.
Never visited the AA
Cos when you drink you go cra-zay.

If you got a problem, drugs won't solve 'em
They won't dissolve 'em.
You'll hit rock bottom
These are things to consider, when you take drugs.

LSD like DMT like BZP
Don't wanna have to get your stomach pumped.
Yellow Submarine, little bit of codeine,
Methamphetamine.

I heard that I had been in quite the state
My friends all hate me cos I brought my mate.
This is becoming quite a problem
Plus I keep waking up with chronic runs.

Booze, Pills, Cactus made me vomit on the couch
I took some Speed and chewed off half my mouth.
I can't keep livin' life at this pace
Snorting lines my nose fell off my face.

Cos I didn't listen when they say
You really need to go and pay, aye.
Never visited the AA
Cos when you drink you go cra-zay.

If you got a problem, drugs won't solve 'em
They won't dissolve 'em.
You'll hit rock bottom
These are things to consider, when you take drugs.

Like San Pedro, *"I'm in love with the Coco"*
El' smoko.
You're gonna have to get your stomach pumped
Three bottles of wine complimented with a couple of lines.

Be-sides, it is a crime
These are things to consider when you take drugs.

~ (25) 21 July 2015.

See video: https://youtu.be/2QIiMyEaZPE

"'shrooms" - magic mushrooms that induce hallucinations.
"Coco" -cocaine.
"Couple of lines" - shorting cocaine on glass arranged in parallel lines to be
    induced with a straw along the line.

Aristotle in the Dark

One looks up at night and what does one see?
The Ancients saw a dark dome pricked by holes
Through which leaked the light of god-knows what?
–Divinity?

Aristotle had no idea, as his cough wracked his
Ailing frame and rheumatism,
Pricked his joints.
–Knowledge.

We've walked upon the moon and know
That out beyond, stars are exploding balls of gas and colour
Debris –hurled like shotgun pellets through space and time.
–Mass.

What is the blackness between the stars?
Is it stuff? Is it the default of nothingness?
Yet black is something.
– Vacuum.

Trillions of exploding nuclear fusion reactions
Going off; suspended in all that empty blackness.
Can the vacuum blackness be the lights beyond the stars?
Their colour well back beyond, but converging?

And generations of stars behind them, their light converging
And generations behind those converging.
All coming at us at once between the gaps of what we see?
The light massed together as a wall of blackness?

But when colour combines, doesn't it turn white?
Isn't light white, and its children rainbow hues?
Why then isn't the night sky white behind the light and the
colour of the stars' messengers that have reached our eyes?

No, the black vacuum of space cannot be layers upon layers
of generations of galaxies of orbs and fusion
Beyond what we can see; exploding and sending their light
to us. They must be things suspended in blackness.

Space must be some sort of default template in to which are
scattered things unmeasurable, untouchable, indiscernible –
yet, black. The perfect baseboard for God to swing a
majesty of lights for us to see when we look up.

There is no center to space or the universe
It depends on where you are.
And think about where it ends.
Does it just go and go beyond comprehens.?

Can it stop? An end? An end of what? Whiteness?
Nothing? But white is a thing –light converged. And so we
spin, suspended –real and actual– within a Great Unreal.
Beyond comprehension and defying definition.

And Aristotle coughed.
Scratched out his fire
Sending tiny embers swirling up to the ceiling on the hot
rising air. Like tiny stars in a room of blackness.

~ (55) 2017.

Pink Polo Freestyle
[before hittin' South Korea].

They hear me rappin,' they be like *"Damn plough"*
"Al Stringer going ham plough."

They always be like *"Man he a homo.*
Look at that fool –He wear a pink po-lo."
Yeah f**k it, I just do what I want,
I 'm a keep it one hunnard when I chill at the spot.

I must keep rappin,' I got spaghetti in my hair
I look like *Calvin Klein* under-wear (male model).
Now I'm drinkin' the bottle
I just gotta do it and I'm scrappin' mah bottle, chillin.'

I got pizza, I listen to Bob Dylan, I'm all in ya kitchen
And I'm feelin' like Ben Stiller.
No body has been iller.
My beard used to be furrier than a chinchilla.
But now I look 12 years old and I'm just chillin.'
I'm so old, my balls are growin' mould (check it out!)

I don't know what I be spittin.' This is freestyle.
This is some crazy sh-t I ain't written.
But I'm contradict-ing everything that I spit when I sittin'
Inside ya kitchen, and you know I be flippin' them lyrics,
Damn.

I'm sober as hell, I'm knocking at your door
I'm like *"Jehovah is well."*
If you remember to take Patrick Gower's butt chin and times
it by 12.

You get the f**king meaning to life.
And the life goes on, but I'm gonna keep it one hunnard.
"I'm just smokin' the bomb," Nah.

I smokin' spiffs and drinkin' piss, I'm getting' chonged
Yeah you know I'm a gen-i-us, when it comes to the song
They wanna hear me flow.
I'm on the road I'm outta hear like, Woh.

They ain't got the sh-t I got .
They can't keep it hot from the sh-t that I drop.
I'm straight chokin,' I ain't smokin,' I'm on the e-ciggie.
Because I was broke when I used to smoke
Them cigarettes. I look like *Superman*, I got a bag flappin'
out the back of my arse.

Whaddam I sayin'? I should give up this freestyle rap,
It just straight-up sux.
*"Look at you Stringer, you a f**kin' mess –look how you
dress! You f***kin fool!"* Nah.

I just love rappin.' I love takin' sh-ts, I love crappin.'
I don't know what I'm on, but I'm just keepin' it together
For the sake of the song.
And now it's three minutes and it's OUT.

OUT to South Korea, Yeah no doubt!
That's what life is all about.
Gonna do it now, I'm outta this bitch like chow.
Catch-ya later, Yeah.

~ (25) 29 December 2016.

See video: https://www.youtube.com/watch?v=UhelQrtoLM8

"Ham/man plough" -male appendage; 'ploughing fields,' 'sowing wild oats;'
  so "Damn plough" would be 'that damn male workin' it,' 'ploughing on.'
"Bomb" - doing it or using a bottle like implement to smoke drugs (bong).
"Hunnard" - $100, the full quid, full amount as in legit. Doing it 100%.
"Spittin'" - putting out a rap as in *"flippin' them lyrics."*
"Spliff" - self-roll cigarettes; marijuana and tobacco mixed.
"Chonged" - high like *Cheech & Chong.*
"E-ciggie" - smoking implement that uses flavoured water vapour.

A-A-Alliteration Song

If there's one thing I learned while I was in school
    Is that a-llit-er-a-tion it is cool.

Bernie the Belligerent Bastard was burning
    bibles in the back of the Buick because
        the babies with the boobies believed.

Cory the carnivorous cookie consumer
    Constantly calculated curriculum and
        Clearly couldn't con-ceive.

Lilly the librarian lost a lot of the lemons
    When the losers let the lions lick the lesbians
        When Larry would leave

Nigel the Neanderthal nailed the naked neighbour
    Knowing that Nathan negotiated naïve.

If there's one thing I learned while I was in school
    Is that a-llit-er-a-tion it is cool.

~ (25) 25 January 2016.

See video: https://youtu.be/zyufXnlv2-w

Begat the Mule

A mule is an an-i-mal !
        Not quite a horse or a donkey
           Nor an ass.

And humbly carries the burdens of life
        Up rocky trails of strife
           The workhorse of humanity.

And on a mule the pagan prophet Balaam sat,
        Saved by a mule
           With eyes to see an Angel of Death.

And on a mule Mary sat,
        And begat,
           A Saviour!

And on a Mule that Saviour sat,
        And begat,
           A King!

And when heaven and earth are renewed,
        Will not the Christ a special place create,
           For the mule who bore him thence?

Along with Dove and Fish of Galilee,
        Lamb and Lion (of Judah),
           Where no Eagles of Rome or Nap-o-leon

Are permitted to be!

~ (55) September 2017.

Equus africanus asinus

Fame does not Sustain:
Reflection on Robert Falcon Scott

Captain Robert Falcon Scott's gargantuan epic beyond human endurance and his marshalling of good men to death, driven by his fear of the mundane and the melancholia that accompanies it; the sentence to insignificance; and the need to transcend; "*achieve!*" be remembered. The latter his ticket out of the mundane forever.

But note the enormous achievement of Lewis and Clark After which –NOTHING– So Lewis blew his brains out on a porch in Alaska.

Fame does not sustain. It is a treadmill. Thus the abuses of Hollywood; the attention-seeking of celebrity; and the suicide of unhappiness (Robin Williams). The overdosing of Phillip Seymour; Heath Ledger; Amie Winehouse~ or the depression of Mel Gibson.

Paul: *"Wretched man that I am, who will deliver me from this body of death? Thanks be to Jesus Christ the author and finisher of my faith."* He understood from the beginning.

The author of Hebrews: *"Since the children have flesh and blood, he too shared in their humanity so that by his death he might break the power of him who holds the power of death—that is, the devil—*
...For this reason he [was] made like them, fully human in every way."

~ (55) Jan 2016.

On the occasion of Cpt. Scott's commemorative statue, made by his wife, being returned to public view at Quake City in Christchurch after the 2010/2011 earthquakes prior to its re-installation on the Avon, Worcester St.

Ed Sheeran Remix
– Things You Don't Wanna Say to the Missus

Ba-by I'm right!
Ba-by you're wrong!
It's pla-in to see.
So why don't you g-o
Cook me a fee-d, I'm really hung-ry.
This is one good way to lose your girl.
So Ba-by can't you see, I'm watchin' TV?
Yes, you do look real fat in your brand new jeans
I think you've put on a few kay gees [kgs].
(thinking out loud) That's the per-fect way to lo-se your girl.

~ (25) 01 January 2016.

See video: https://youtu.be/puF-ZUazvoU

Life Shade

How come if life is Blue
       I'm always in the Red.
Fighting Black and Blue
       To earn a few,
While family and friends
       Are adieu?

Life Greys
       To autumn Hue
Amid time's dew
       –due to you (and me)–
Sheltered 'neath
       That tall life tree!

~ (55) 23 October 2016.

Make Time for Play

You don't wanna be bitten by one of the most
            venom-ous bugs
'makes you sit at your desk in your suit and drink
            from your coffee cup.
Workin' day in an' day out, never quite makin' enough.
            Submittin' to the machine
                    Never doin' what you love.

When you were younger, you never realised
            this is what it was.
Now you're older and you're not in the world you was
            dreamin' of.
If you don't want life to steal your soul a-waay
            You gotta make time for pl-aay.
                    Make time for pl-aay.

Doesn't matter what you're in to or what you think
            that you love.
You might be into dancing with hermaphrodites
            at the club.
You might be into bathing with your favourite
            rubber duck
You might be into going to the beach
            with people you love.
You should do whatever you wanna
            as long as you're not a, country-destroying hater
                    Who looks down on people from above.

Just remember, that if you're only working,
            it's not enough.
Don't let 'the man' bend you over,
            cos he will try take you up.
It's a well-oiled machine and sometimes
            I feel it's co-rrupt.

Don't let it bug you down,
        you just gotta have some fun.

Have a party!
        Go get wild!
Try and channel your in-ner child.
        Cos you gotta remember what it's like to feel
            You're alive.

Sometimes you can turn into a zombie
        with that nine to five.
Surround yourself with people
        who recipro-cate a good vibe.
Now you're chillin' with some homies
        and you're havin' a good time.
Don't let yourself become a robot
        of bureau-cratic li-fe.

Try and remember the child
        that you are on the in-side.
If you don't want life to steal your soul a-waay
        Make timc for pl-aay.

~ (25) 24 January, 2016.

See video: https://youtu.be/cv3fHnj3hYl

"Chillin' with some homies" - relaxing with friends.

Spare a Dime?

"Spare a dime?"
      The corner man cries.
You can tell he's broken
      By the look in his eyes.
A man of many riches
      His nose in the air.
Walks on by
      He doesn't care.
Behind him walks a poor girl
      Who throws down a coin.
And for competition's sake
      He throws down nine.
He then says to the poor man
      "Who do you prefer?
"A man who gives you plenty?
      Or a ragged bum like her?"
He looks toward the poor girl
      The rich man looks mad.
Sure he gave the most
      But the girl gave all she had.

~ (25). The Widow's Mite, Luke 21:1 -4.

After Phil Collins: *Another Day in Paradise*, 1989.

"She calls out to the man on the street/ "Sir, can you help me?
It's cold and I've nowhere to sleep/ Is there somewhere you can tell me?"

"He walks on, doesn't look back/ He pretends he can't hear her
Starts to whistle as he crosses the street/ Seems embarrassed to be there.

"You can tell from the lines on her face/ You can see that she's been there
Probably been moved on from every place/ 'Cos she didn't fit in there."

Otautahi Eight (Rakaia 222)

1. Sky stretches azure-blue forever.

2. Hot norwester blows
      and weeping willows groan.

3. Chirping orchestra of gold finches
      cavorts in a Canterbury
            conifer windbreak.

4.'Rivers' flow across hot dry
            asphalt mirages
                  while insects staccato
                        windscreen and air.
5. Sheep pant.
      Sparrows play
            Twister in the dust.
                  Washing flaps and lines strain.
                        Uprights rock to and fro, Wells' Tripods.

6. Where tied fly whisks on line 'cross placid pool
      While trout hunker down lazily 'neath bank
            Wrapped in weed, where koura gropes
                  And feels a way, a universe away
                        From lobster, conger
                              or coral sea, cousins thrice removed.
7. Kaitorete surf crashes down
      On shingle and sand,
            And grinds them back again, to glass
                  Above the bones of Ngati Mamoe, all gone.
                        Kete baskets empty now
                              But harakeke stands vigil
                                    Sentinel of centuries.

8. Where Father Norwester blows and has blown
      Warm embrace across –willow, conifer, road and field
            Washing line, river way, sea beach,
                  Whipping across shingle sand,
                        While harakeke stand of nodding stalks,
                              Windblown quivering green blades–
                                    Winding time into skin and limb,
                                          Water, tree and rock, as tags of forever.
~ (55) 07 November 2019.

Androgynous A and Androgynous B

Androgynous A and Androgynous B
      Went up the hill to fetch a pale of H_2O.
Androgynous A fell down and broke its crown and
      Androgynous B came tumbling after
[in order to be equal in all things].

Up they got [together, so neither would be seen
      to be pre-eminent]
And home did trot to their mutually owned co-habitation
      [in terms of the *Matrimonial Properties Act*, 1976]
As fast as they could caper.

They went to be bed
      Where Androgynous A bandaged its own head
[because Androgynous B should not be seen in a
      subservient servant role]
With vinegar and a culturally safe blend of white, yellow
      And brown [recycled] paper.

~ (55) April 1995.

Otautahi Eight *(Rakaia III)*

"Otautahi" (Maori) for part of the area around Christchurch, New Zealand.
"Rakaia" - large braided river south of Christchurch.
"Harakeke" - (Maori) flax.
"Ngati Mamoe" - New Zealand South Island tribe, destroyed by Ngai Tahu.
"Koura" - (Maori) fresh water crayfish.
Kaitorete - long shingle coast south of Banks Peninsula with crashing surf.
"Kete" - bag woven from harakeke.

You Can Find It Online

You can find any-thing you need,
On the World Wide Web, is where people be.
Human-ity's knowledge with a quick con-nection.

But it can also be a pre-tty dark place,
Because it's not like you are face-to-face,
You should see the a-buse in the *YouTube*
comm-ents sec-tion.

An-y ridiculous abstract concept you can think of
in your mind. You can find it online!

Tactical photography from fat chicks,
To make 'em appear thinner in their profile pics,
Dwarves riding mini-ature ponies in sl-ow mo-tion.

You can get a pizza delivered to your house,
You can buy silver or may-be your spouse;
Re-search the aliens that live in the deep o-cean.

An-y in-sane thought that you can muster up
inside your mind. You can find it online!

I'll tell you something that ain't the best,
People that keep sending me game requests.
Take your *Pirate Quest* bollocks and go a-way.

You can find a video of a mannequin's rap,
Google your symptoms for a pan-ic a-ttack,
Or you can buy a plane ticket to Zim-bab-wae.

An-y ridiculous abstract concept you can think of
in your mind. You can find it on line!

~ (25) 2016.

See video: https://youtu.be/8m-ieoKwVaA

Winston Peters Rap
– Pre(Eminem)t of the PM Leaders

[Set to some appropriated rowing music of *Eminen*].

My name is Win-ston Pe-ters
      Pre-(*Eminen*)t of the Lea-ders
I gave Bolger/the cold shoulder
      Sank HMS Shipley.

They call me "*Gucci*" or "*Luigi*"
      But I'll give them some El Ducé,
A 'D-Day' on E-Day
      Al Alamein up their jacksy.

Those "*shiny bums*" spend all your funds,
      Leave you in the slums,
So I gave you the Gold Card, it's gone plati-num,
      While they sleazed up to you for a sum.

I'm the 'Hunua Goer;'
      Want the Regions of New Zealand back in clover
Manu-fact-uring and some dairy
      But not to foreign nationals, that's scary.

"*Happy to be the MP for Tau-ranga!*"
      I was the people's political monger.
Got the call-up for hometown North-land
      While National had its head-in-the-sand.

If I'm the New Zealand 'Trump,' I'll deal some cards
      I'll do 'em all in political poker,
Cos I'm the Joker – of the people
      I don't smoke, but I'm smokin.'

I drink – from a Wine Box
      I gave the pox to those elitist folks

'Fay Rich Rights' but they're wrong
    So they're gone; got no gong.

Kim Dot-Con, the German crim. with the grin
    Whether you're Maori or Euro-pe-an,
Makes no difference to me; Ho-ne.
    Bill English. I'm Scottish-Irish. But nobody's perfect.

I draw from across the board,
    Cos the voters are bored with
Labour-Green-National, let's be factual
    2% population growth, 1% GDP – that's no hope.

I'm happy under FPP or MMP
    Makes no difference to me.
I've called in Jonesy, a whirlwind for Whangarei
    He'll make the Nats pay, all the way to E-Day.

My name is Win-ston Pe-ters
    A political phoenix, tearin' the other parties to pieces
Chinese or Czechoslovakian.
    You're welcome.

But you gotta come sec-ond
    To New Zealanders first.
Jobs and training for our people, that's our religious steeple
    Then you're the add-in, all ten thous-and.

Metiria says I'm racist.
    That's just fascist. She fell off the List.
Benefit 'fraudster,' public trougher.
    Politically green; I'll make them Green with en-vy.

They'll be two binding referendum
    Let the people speak on some–
Important issues, that they care about
    Come 23 September they'll have some clout.

Labour and the Greens will Peters out.
       I'll give them such an MMP whipping,
They'll have as many stripes
       As my pin-stripe *Gucci* slip-on.

Don't listen to the hype,
       Of the fake news liberal tripe.
I'm Winston Pe-ters, pre-(*Eminen*)t of the Lea-ders.
       We're comin' for the center.

Backing New Zealand to be better
       Our people first,
That's no fantasy
       You'll see come September 23.

~ (55) September 2016.

"El Ducé" - Mussolini.
"Jacksy" - up ya bum/bottom.
"Wine box" - famous political scandal that made Peter's career.
"Hunua Goer" - Peters entered parliament after winning a successful
    judicial review of the Hunua electorate votes in 1979.
"Hone" - MP for Northland John Carter (were peters later stood) often went
    on Talkback Radio disguised as "Hone."
"Jonesy - Hon Shane Jones.
"Metiria" - Metiria Turei disgraced Greens co-leader.
"Trougher" - living off public funds like pigs to swill in a trough.
"E-Day" - election day.

See last page.

Ahead of the general election 23 September 2016 amidst wide speculation as to whom Winston Peter's and NZFirst would coalesce with to form a potential 2016 government. Postscript: NZF eschewed National party of the most votes and formed a majority coalition with Labour and the Greens.

There's Rules While Smoking Weed (Beyonce Remix)

To the left, to the left…To the left, to the left…
Pass that joint to the dude on your left.
It's going clock-wise, don't stuff it up, cos
I'm re-ally keen to get a puff.

A good yarn is al-ways fine,
But can you yarn and smoke at the same time?
Cos it's my weed that's in that 'J'
So hurry up, I ain't got all day.

Something that does bug me,
Which people don't seem to un-der-stand,
0.85 ain't the same thing as-a gra-m. Got me to say…

There's rules while smokin' weed.
There's rules while smokin' weed.
Just hit it twice, then you pa-ss it.
It ain't that hard, you silly bast-ard! Ba-by.

There' s rules while smokin' weed.
There' s rules while smokin' weed.
Don't get the ciggie wetter than the Pacific!
You hit it not French Kiss it! Ba-by.

So let's go get stoned.
Light the spliff, pack the dang bong.
I have not forgot you're hooked up bro,'
Whaddya think I was rollin' a blunt for?

Cos you know me, ya gotta spread love
With the buds to your hom-ies.
That's what I do. And you should really do
The same thing too.

People that are happy to par-take in a pu-ff
Yet they don't ever pro-vide
Their own stuff.
It's got me to say…

There's rules while smokin' weed.
There's rules while smokin' weed.
You hit it not French Kiss it! Ba-by.
Don't get the ciggie wet-ter than the Pacific! Ba-by.

~ (25) 2015.

See video: htttps://youtu.be/H2RSsGuJpqE

"ciggie wet-ter" - don't overly moisten the end of the shared cigarette.
"spliff" - a marijuana cigarette with tobacco in it.

St Pauls' Papanui

Beautifully fitted wooden beams and buttresses from trees
cut down in 1850, soaring still above worshipful bowed
heads, murmured prayers through the branches of life.

The gravestones of the faithful who have gone before,
clustered round the church as a phalanx of limestone
warriors, a sacred ring of standing stones.

Fallen leaves patter down each autumn to accompany
Wednesday and Sunday pealing bells of the wooden-
clothed carillon, ringing out "*the Past is Present*!"

Cups of tea, Christmas tree, moral-ity, in the lee,
of a world gone nuts over sex and identity, self vs
community, service vs vice, and vice-versity.

St Paul stares down with Pre-Raphaelite austerity, lit by light
from nature's glow through the win-dow of this sanctuary,
positing slivers of colour on each sacred face.

Springing child, hoary head, man in prime, woman aglow,
the community of saints gathered in song, in prayer, in liturgy
illuminated via lithium glow screen.

Weathered pews of oiled wood, worn smooth by generations
of passing holy hands, a nest around eggs: a blue hymnal, a
bible, a prayer book, keys, a cellphone.

St Paul's Papanui. Gathering place of spiritus sanctus doves
of flight, light, life and love amidst trees long gone, a forest of
faith soaring up as the cathedral of this place.

~ (55).On the occasion of the parish's special AGM, 9 September 2018
that divided the congregation over same-sex blessings in the Anglican
church in Aotearoa, New Zealand and Polynesia.

Wellington Railway Station

Indifferent and disaffected yet moving in unison
      Always the same way.
Tramp tramp tramping down the dripping draughty
      Grey-toned funnel we call the subway.
Each to our own wee box,
      A daily container,
While a bracing wind and the salt of the sea
      Calls from unattended wilderness.

And the soil yearns for tending fingers and the feet of a man
      To sing with it,
A symphony of invigoration,
      That echoes distantly in the ears,
As eyes focus on the desk, the telephone
      And the sheets of paper –always the sheets of
      paper–
That men hunt and attack with their modern spear,
      A *BIC Metal Point Roller.*

~ (55) 1992.

"Stand fast among the beam-like spears!"

~ Archilochus, *Poems*, ca 640 BC.

"Soul to Squeeze" Freestyle Remix Feat
[with Jim Stringer first take]

Me – and Jim – comin' on in,
About to spring a rap with a tilted brim, check-it!
It's just how it go, playin' some *Chillies*
Gotta keep it the flow, Yeah.

I'm gonna spit a little rap
But Jim be a big boy bouncin' on the Gap,
So don't try touch me,
I'll kick your face like *Heihachi.*

You know what it is.
It would make your grandmother straight jizz,
So homie just stop it.
Your mother, she looks like Mike McRoberts.
And this is a rhyme; this is the reason I do it.
Cos I not committing to crime.
I sing a little song, I'm out here in Korea,
In Incheon, *"where I go I just don't know."*
I'm about to try and f**king spit a flow.
Big boy Jim plays on the Gap
While we get drunk and record some rap.

Yo. I look kinda crazy
They always [brrrp] *"Stringer why doncha
join the damn navy!*
You kinda acting like a ba-by.
You kinda acting [flikkada wikkada] crazy!"
Cos I'm tryna be sober, I'm a [pikkada pikkada] pav-lova.
It's just how it goes.
Keep it one hunnard when I try and spit a flow.
We in Incheon tryin' ta sing a song.
Tryna keep cool,
Away from the bongs.

So hit the chorus one time,
So I can show you mother f**kers how to spin a rhyme.
'Where I go I just don't know
I'm gonna go somewhere I just don't know."

~ (25) 2000.

With James Stringer, Incheon, South Korea.

"Jizz" - ejaculate, thus *"make even your grandmother have an orgasm"* or
   be so excited they pee their pants.
"flikkada wikkada, pikkada pikkada" - phonetics.
"Chillies" - the *Red Hot Chilly Peppers*, a band.
"Heihachi" Mishima - a character in a Namco's Tekken kung-fu type game.
"Hunnard" - $100, the full quid, full amount as in legit. Doing it 100%.

The Wind

The wind moves like a ribbon,
Screaming at the window,
Begging to be let in as he is waiting
Like a howling dingo.

Charges like a bulldog,
Ripping up the trees,
Skimming the waterbed
Making people freeze.

The next morning his job is done.
Because he ripped up trees,
Blew down fences and was
Scared away by the fog.

~ (10) James, 2000, aged 10.

Alex's second oldest brother.

The Poets

*The family that writes together
is right together.*

~ (55). 2018.

Left to right: Alex (now 25), John (55) and James Stringer (27).

Alex Stringer in Christchurch with the Rt Hon. Winston Peters, New Zealand deputy prime minister, 2017, "pre-(*Eminem*)t of the Leaders."

See poems on: p. 50; also 15, 19.

www.ingramcontent.com/pod-product-compliance
Lightning Source LLC
Chambersburg PA
CBHW061441050726
47637CB00002B/9